AF413616

Photography & Journals
by Brian Greenwald

Patina

Patina

Patina

Strong waves crash upon the
land of the free. A French gift
of patina strikes my eyes, as I
stand hopelessly trying to find
comfort in this inanimate object.
I'm fifteen, and trekked all
the way from New Jersey with my
father to find solace within a
dream. I had never seen the city
of chaotic hope, but I had always
wondered what pulled in the
masses.

As I stare up at the woman I
had only seen through history
pages, my teachers have force-
fully projected onto my screens,
I can't help but think;How brave
she must be.The things she has
seen. Lived a million lives
in a million New York cities.
What wrongs she has seen. What
triumphs she's endured. Her
patina speaks volumes. I fear
I might still be a brightly
colored copper. A mere penny
in hand.

The land I stand on; One house.
One childhood. a few versions
of New Jersey. Many more to come.

I think patina scares me.

Patina

Patina is the land I stand on.
New Jersey's copper dwindles
within the cracks of my memories,
but the green like moss covers
all my youthful mud that once
allowed me to shine. I fear I've
lost what this place meant to me.
I fear the patina sends shock
waves to my system, and I must
find the tiniest bit of copper
I once knew to be true.

Patina

I forgive my patina. I shine
light on the aquamarine green-
like state of being. I advertise
it now to send a wider audience
to bear witness to such extra-
ordinary defeat. I'll tell
everyone where I came from. I
don't know why, but it feels
like the best way to describe
myself
my art
my writing.

I allow my patina to speak for
me. I'm bored of trying to find
some sort of reason to push away
something that allowed me to
paint green on my copper canvas.
Stretched the shit out of it
onto wooden panels that start
to tremble, as I re-staple the
fabric to continue my long
awaited masterpiece.

I sit in a field of green. Won-
dering how I felt at fifteen.
I thought there was nothing for
me here. I thought venturing out
would answer a billion questions.
I didn't even know what I was
trying to ask. She looked down
at me, with aqua eyes.

— Why are you here so soon? Wait
a few years. You'll know what to
ask then.

She was right.
I go back every now and then to
visit a friend. To visit the
coffee shops I love to pretend
in. Pretend I'm city folk just
like them. Pretend I belong to
the rampage of overdetermined
crowds. I still don't know where
I'm headed when I join the
business men for a dance, but at
least I understand. I understand
the purpose. I understand why I
need to feel the need to run.

But as I sit in this field, in
Haddon Heights New Jersey, I
finally feel comfort where I
came. I remember how it felt to
feel nothing in the midst of a
sun shower, and to feel every-
thing in the shadows of these
bush-filled trees. I sit in my
patina, hoping to wonder once
more, how it feels
                    to   run.

Winona calls me from Philly.
— I knew he would cancel again.

Patina

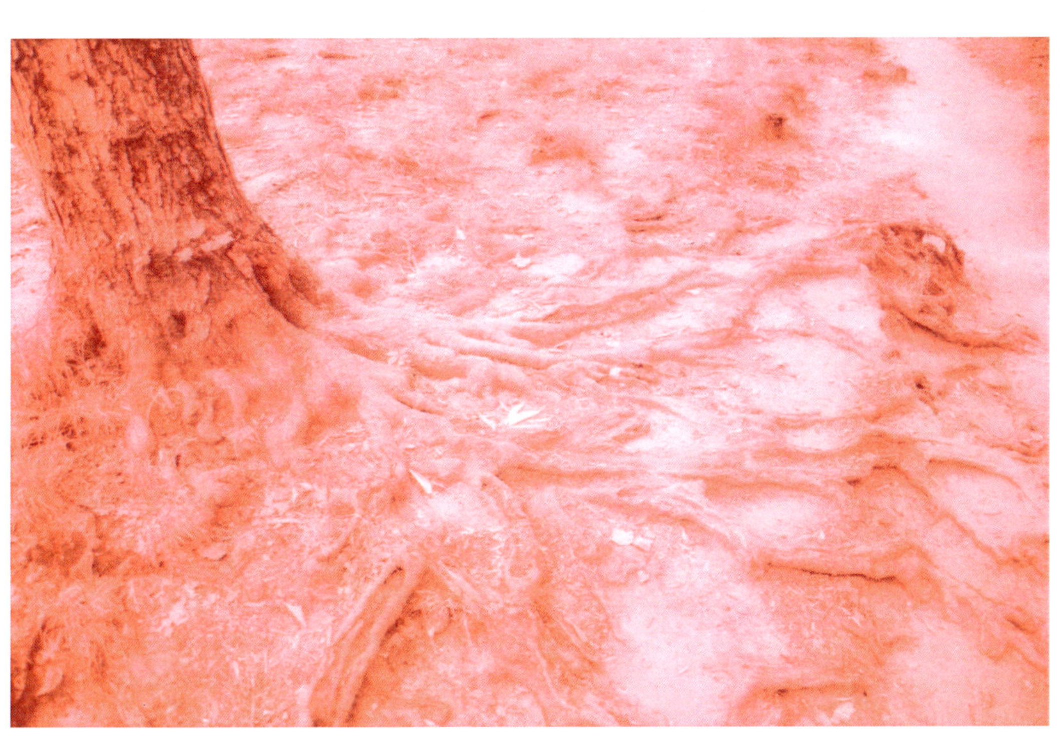

— I love it. It's the kinda book
  that inspires me to write.

I say to some new man I met through
landlines I constantly intertwine.

I speak of new found wonderings
and lost hope, that sinks beneath
newly paved slabs of concrete at
the house sitting on the corner
of my hometown street.

I grow tired of the blurry words
on devices I replace every couple
years. Gratefully so, but there
was a time when I didn't have to
speak into an endless void of un-
passionate circumstance.

—Just look at your phone
and answer my fucking text.

a countless amount of times I've
said that out loud about a man
I've never met.

As I sit in Jersey, in a dining
room that has changed appearance
many times, I crave the escape
once more. Just like when I was
twelve and needed the shore, and
when I was 18 and ran to New
York. Only lasted a month there,
but still.

I call up my mother and we flee
the scene.

Patina

Ocean City lays there, as it
always has. Thank god.

I breathe in the salty atmosphere
I've swam in for nearly two
decades now. I take in the
patience from my mom and allow
the seagulls to be the only
ones with an "on edge, eagerness"
to run.

As I stare into the ocean, I spot
a dense figure in my periphery.
A quick glance now turns into a
long stare.

Burnt sienna watercolor.
Sunlit highlights bouncing off
bulging craters.

A quick glance from a statue
that hadn't yet lost its vivid
shine.
A surfer.

The delusions sink in
as my desire lingers.

Then I remember.
I'm with my mother.

I wonder if Frankenstein
had any regrets
Maybe I should find out
A black white noir to teach me
about a "fait-filled" night

Some point in time,
     mid July

Hide me on the shores of

          Babylon.

C. EUGENE MILLER, M. D.
Ephrata, Pa.
W. Main St.
Take
Drops
Teaspoons
Tablespoons
Every
Times

Patina

I carry the weight of them on my
back. Historical nonsense happens
to interject.

What came from the yester-years?

How does Mary push down the
domino that pushes another
until I need to push myself

                       to move
                              forward?

Strength came from the feminine
urge to ~~love.~~
to ~~hold~~
to scream.

Confidence that exudes through
experience I haven't had the
chance to explore. I see it
through their eyes, though.

Marianne tries to carry the weight
of the women that had held her
up high. Her strength trickles
down onto me, and I feel the
power that comes from one's who
nurture.

Patina

I listen to them and observe.
They don't dwindle on murcurial
changes, because they've already
seen how the world has trans-
formed. A non-stop battle between
the past and the future.

Their faces are my google search
answer, as it was their thesaurus
referense.

Patina

Now I write my own journals,
and reflect on what's mine.

The
end

Patina

www.ingramcontent.com/pod-product-compliance
Lightning Source LLC
Chambersburg PA
CBRC090518160726
48196CB00090B/733